IN HER SHAMBLES

to all my family, my baby boy Jack
and The Spoke

IN HER SHAMBLES

Elizabeth Parker

Seren is the book imprint of
Poetry Wales Press Ltd.
57 Nolton Street, Bridgend, Wales, CF31 3AE
www.serenbooks.com
facebook.com/SerenBooks
twitter@SerenBooks

ISBN: 978-1-78172-446-0
ebook: 978-1-78172-447-7
Kindle: 978-1-78172-448-4

A CIP record for this title is available from the British Library.

The publisher acknowledges the financial assistance of the Welsh Books Council.

Cover artwork: 'Edie', Collage on Paper by Maria Rivans
www.mariarivans.com

Printed in Bembo by Airdrie Print Services Ltd.

Contents

Crockery

I can't look at you. I keep my eyes on crockery
notice you are split between glass, chrome, china
your index finger a pink glow in the saltcellar's skirt
face a pale glaze on white plates.

The wine glass has peeled a crescent from your mouth
each crease ridging the grease. I can't look at you.
Instead, I watch your coffee ripple
when you knock the table with a knee.

As you leave, glasses clear
spoons lose their dash of colour.

Rescues

Fallow doe caught in the boundary fence
fetlock trapped in the top straining wires

wind plucking her fur
as my father squeezed wire cutters
until they bit, freed her to bolt
streak into bracken.

Barely-there weight of the pipistrelle
he scooped from the outdoor loo
as if a bit of night had torn away
wafted through.

Their roost in the unused loft
tucking through 'the wrong hole'
shadows in ceiling corners
black fruits he gently unpeeled
to show us wings laced with limb.

House martin chicks fledging early
from the mud bowl of the nest
spit-wattled to rafter and wall
too keen to muscle for flight

picked from gaps in stacked compost pallets
'soft tickle on your palm'
the texture of breath
heartbeats batting his hand.
'There's nothing there. No weight in them.
Same with anything that flies.'

His gloved hands
click-locking a step ladder
placing them back in the wrong nest
hoping they'd be adopted.

Birds, shrews, mice
pried from the white portcullis
of the cat's teeth

tiny bump of their pulse
on his fingertips
thimble hearts pumping
final millilitres of blood.

Black bathtub spiders
peeping legs through gaps
in the tunnel of his thick tan fingers.

A fractured buzzard
by Cannop Brook
cowled in a bath towel.

His three daughters
calling to him from their cities
shrill cry of the phone
his voice, still Brummie-soft,
saving us each time.

Clasp

She scrunches onion paper
pinches a tooth of garlic from its husk.
One of the first absences she noticed was a missing scent.

Morning skies are thinning more quickly
like our ghosts thin, she thinks, in daylight.

There is a time with the curtains drawn
when the white ceiling they painted together
twitches with worms, scribbles, dots of light.

She puts more garlic in the food now
notices her shadow alone on the walls
writes with that pencil he enjoyed
yellow and thick as a finger

awkward, slippy lead that blunts quickly
no sharpener big enough
so she pares it with his clasp knife
peels its nib

wood curling to ringlets
lead peppering her palm.

Sipped

As the Sunday city turns from light, you're burning weeds,
blackberry torn from a barbed fence,
snarls of wire and stem.

Brambles sprinkle your arms with nicks.
Dead plants are sharpest – no sap softening their claws.

When you return, I pick hooks from your coat,
tresses of stickyweed from your hair.

You rub a gleam of ointment on stung arms,
your mum's homemade balm –
dock leaves pummelled for sap,
mashed with Vaseline.

I bow to your puncture wounds,
touch lips to scribbles on your skin.

Squeezing brown juices from jeans,
a wool jumper seasoned with smoke,
I lay your peelings on a radiator.

The air is brothy with steam,
gasps of greasy heat from the oven
where a chicken is sweating to a crisp.

Following Lavinia

Who is this? My niece that flies away so fast!
                    Marcus, 'Titus Andronicus'

I. John

I spent a summer reading the Roman plays aloud
in a yellow attic room in Coventry
after John moved out.

I read the hunt while spotting grazes on paint
pale patches on the carpet
mapping where his furniture stood

sitting at his desk
sinking nails into polish and wax
from candles he'd burnt

plugged into wine bottles
drooling trails
that cooled and whitened.

I read the hunt
gathering flakes beneath my nails.

II. Neil

I watched the hunt in Edinburgh
from a stall which smelt of polish.

A friend's fringe debut.

I had seen actors rush, spit, edit
but Neil laid the lyric gently on her cheek
refused to cut her uncle's elegy
to her limbs, her voice.

III. Paul

I watched the hunt with Paul
on a pull-down screen
in a Warwick lecture theatre

desktops soft enough
to sink a pencil tip in veneer
scratch my name.

Paul was hung-over
left on the shot where they staked her out
on silvered wetland

her new language
scribbling from her mouth
her wrists
her fluent heart.

IV. Their Names

*She takes the staff in her mouth, and guides it with
her stumps, and writes.*
                              'Titus Andronicus'

They took her tongue, her hands
so she tried to write with driftwood, sand.

The sea was too strong
her words little caves water curled up in
blunting their edges.

She tried to speak again
carved deeper.

The sea was proud with storm
collapsed their walls
blanked the beach
to a nonsense of weed

silenced the sand.

Hands

On the bus two women show each other their hands
brush one finger along another

pause above a joint to strum creases
in skin they've worn so long
they admire and grieve the time it keeps

tap a cross-hatch of wrinkles
trace stitcheries of blood
tut at a crinkled knuckle.

We watch those hands
pause our eyes on their thumbs.

You rub warm your weak knuckles
a cave of aches every winter
scaly with eczema.

We have flowed,
passed currents through these hands.

The women smile as they chafe
summon blood to glow wintry fingertips.
It is slower these days
they must wait until it obeys.

They interweave fingers in their laps
turn to the window
to boys playing football on a green
with cardboard fruit box goals

but we keep finding new detail in our hands
wrinkles, shallows between ridged veins.

We hadn't noticed this fine work
blood in relief when we turn our wrists
ink-blue and hard.

Quiet Water

She is afraid of quiet water

not the river tearing on slate
when it reaches the falls
but water that sneaks

a pipe bent up from mud
its leak snaking through oatgrass and deadnettle
twitching each stem

a culvert under bracken
seeping its tiny stream.

Ghosting

I spent a day reading deep water
fish six thousand metres down
making light in their skins.

That night
a squatter climbed into the rusted warehouse
roofed in rippled tin
vaulted the spiked security gate at 3am

slid through an empty window frame
shimmering the roof
flinging storm sounds.

I watched him
as light without source
selected parts of his body.

It was as if he was glowing
making light in his skin.

I still held the afterimage
of the day's page
its glossy ink, flashing fish.

I watched him glow
until all I saw was those fish
flashing, fading

not a man or a blackened warehouse
but memories of deep water
thoughts of fish ghosting through

hatchet fish
hasting nowhere to nowhere

viperfish
firing like a synapse

a comb jelly's vague lines
catching light
scintillating cilia
pigments pulsing
thrills of colour

the urges of a worm eel
sparking its every cell

glass squid
glowing its bell
pumping to hunt

bright impulses
rippling a bristlemouth

until sunlight came
dried my deepwater brain

hinting human, tin, rust

hinting limb, human skin

hinting him.

She Paints Him

fills in his lips with different reds
daubing the brush for a full mouth.

He pales while she mixes a wash
for his skin: cream, watered pink.

She tips a round brush with catchlights,

dips the edge of a filbert
in thinned umber
to define lip ledges
the high line of his cheeks.

She is brief with background
quick sweeps of dilute green
to hint at walls he papered.

His last breath hauls rain,
warmed leather.

She slides a hand beneath him,
finds his shirt soaked in heat
where his blood has pooled.

Paint exhales its linseed.
Colours begin to fix.

Station

and we begin our walk to Waverley
where he will leave me
between iron pillars
on a cold platform.

On Cockburn Street
beside the blue door
of the Southern Cross café
a piper selects an Irish song
of imagined roads.

He blows long notes
from strong lungs
swells the tartan bag
a puddle of loose change
glinting in a flat cap near his feet
as he weaves our last walk
with Kavanagh's ode to Hilda.

On Raglan Road on an autumn day
I saw her first and knew

Even when the busker has shrunk
to a silent stipple
we remember the poem.

I said let grief be an autumn leaf

In the dark booths
of The Hebrides on Market Street
warm skins steam.

I sip the froth
from a black stout

watch his hands
mirrored in ale
knowing he will leave me
with the clunk of locks
along the train.

The deep ravine where can be seen
the worth of passion's pledge

Over the bridge
a Westerly flickers pigeons
on the station's glazed roofs.

O I've loved too much

They lift
quiver air
above panes tinted with algae
framed in dark metal.

and by such, by such

The train seals
slides him to another city.

is happiness thrown away

Waiting for sleep
in a B&B on Hill Street
boxed in puce carpet, bland walls
I hear the last lines
over the hiss of Scottish sleet.

When the angel woos the clay
he'll lose his wings at the dawn of day.

Chatelaine

We recite her words from brochures
lay our reflections on the moats
circling his walls
where she once floated her face.

We read that she was only a woman.
We read that she was never enough
painting a new face every morning.
We recite her.

We have learnt every scrap of her
test her fragments in our mouths
her torn story
lay our reflections on the moats

where it is rumoured
she washed his touch from her hair
head dipped in the freezing mirror
circling his walls.

We touch her rooms
let the walls imprint our palms
pray for crumbs to stick
in the grain of our skin
for motes to float on breath.

Rivers

My father's river has risen
above seams that won't be softened or stolen
from hard lime and coal
to pennant sandstone that gives
until the water is precious
pewter

My sister's river is root beer with rot
the dead giving up their tannins
letting riches from their skins

My grandfather's river floats rafts of flotsam
scum bobs and pops near its walls
He says it has turned from pea to tea
that his favourite part
sometimes flows the wrong way

My friend is afraid
of her river's urge for her

Despite wide-mouthed sewers
my grandmother's river still licks up storms

My mother's river keeps forking
thinning to little more than shine
Her deft eye gathers its frays
slicks them back to their source

My brother's river
broods behind loch gates

My aunt's river grazes its banks
and widens
Rocks are loosed to salt her river

Some drink from their rivers
morsels of light and water
speck their lips

My uncle's river remembers its monks
their nights rowing to secret mass
prows cutting water bonds
to rock chapels in the gorge

My river reaches for me
At night I watch my river
slink toward my feet

Storm water has thickened my grandmother's river
sluicing darkness from the banks

My father's river has broken through
soothes dry mud
allows fish

My friend's river has dropped
can't reach its own watermark
etching of sand that flakes as it dries

This morning my river was high
green and urgent with rain
rushing light and leaves toward the estuary

I have seen it slow
ease its freight of yachts and light

thickened with dark loads

cradling neon

swilling
a dun afternoon

In summer people meet at my river
their bare legs tassel its banks.

White Vase

She bloomed it from the wheel
would not let him near it
knew she'd blame him if she pressed too hard
and had to collapse it, ball it
slam it back.

She threw it
pulled its walls, set the lip
bellied it out, squeezed the top
to close the neck
slathered it with a slip glaze
to seal its skin.

She fired it
clay sintering in her kiln
until its pores shrank.

She never drops his shop bouquets
through its slim neck
only garden flowers and leggy weeds

changes the water every day
their tips snipped of rot, thin hand poured in
to scoop out slimed stem.

Her damp cloth licks up dust
from the only place she can keep unmarked
clean as milk.

Even a window
reflected on its glaze
annoys her.

Lavinia Writes

Sorrow concealed, like an oven stopp'd
Doth burn the heart to cinders where it is.
                    Marcus, 'Titus Andronicus'

I dipped a finger in my mouth
strummed then picked the stitches
in the root of my stolen tongue.

I tipped my head over paper
let my words pump, breach the dam
fill fibres, glut pores.

The page can't hold them any more.
I write bright, long sentences over chairs, walls, floors.

I sign the carpet. It is cleaned.
I write bright, long sentences over chairs, walls, floors.

They sew me up again
offer a fountain pen.

I refuse ink
tear their neat stitcheries.

I sign the carpet. It is cleaned.
I watch pink words sucked by the plughole.

I refuse ink. The carpet stores a stain.
I watch the plughole suck pink water.

I am offered a loom.
A needle is tucked between my teeth.

I am told to weave
a new pattern through the weft.

I am offered a loom, a needle.
I refuse thread, spit the needle.

It falls to the carpet with a red word.
I watch the word creep through the weave.

I tear more, free more
until I am fluent.

Dry

I didn't expect you to breach the dam
loosen my banks until my clay unclenched
dropped its stash of rocks.

You sleeked my snarls of algae
brought a lush hiss to my throat
brown trout wafting their bodies.

You eased my bite
sighs of silt slid
from pebble seams.

I breathed other salts, sediments
floated light
was creamed with moon.

Then you were gone
sun stealing you
leaving me slithers, patches
where my sand tried to keep you

small darknesses tucked beneath my rocks
shrinking day by day.

Sand Cat

To the child staring into your tank
you are nothing more than colours and shapes.

He looks more at the glass than at you,
floats his eye on your eye,

enjoys the ways he overlays you:
his lip over your nose,
his shoulder striped by your banded tail.

Warm air thick in his mouth,
he watches his breath
swell and shrink on Perspex,

doesn't observe the long hairs on your paws
buffering the burn of a desert
trucked in from Cornwall,

your pupils wide for night hunts,
snatching desert larks,
digging out geckos.

You lick your legs,
ready muscles to run
an inch short of the glass,

oversized, fleeced ears
set low to dodge sand never blown,
angled to net surfacing rodents
served dead,

eardrums taut for the tap of insects,
flick-kick of a Cape hare,
dunes popping spiny mice.

You wait for a plain to leak a lizard,
for burrows to whisper *viper*.

You look through light
bursting on the glass,

through the child
misting the pane,

your whole world vague
beneath his breath.

Manus

*It has been proposed that the hominid lineage began
when a group of chimpanzees started to throw rocks
and swing clubs at adversaries.*
                    'The Journal of Anatomy'

I spent the afternoon
reading about our ancient hands
an essay arguing their evolution for use of weapons
not fruit-picking or peaceful tools.

Tonight, *The Observer* on my lap
I watch your rhythmic hands
bridged for *Clair de Lune*
your fingerpads' slight pressure
lifting piano strings.

On the front page
the low-angle shot of an executioner
foregrounds his hand
thumb stabilizing a knife as if to say
'I have whetted blunt flesh.'

*Fingers and thumb form a vice
squeezing the weapon against the palm.*

I follow your piano fingers
honed for three million years.
My skin remembers seduction
you tapped time on my spine
altered my rhythm
lifted fine threads
until my blood re-tuned.

Prehensile grip:
palmaris brevis contracts
stiffens palmar fat pad
cushions knife hilt.

I watch your fine-tuned hands
smooth fingers refined for pixels, paper
for typing, touch screens
buffed soft on spreadsheets
skin and ivory.

Prehensile grip:
Flexor Digitorum flexes
curls your fingers on the keys.

The executioner blazons his hands
to camera phones and paparazzi.
'Look what I have made
of power grip, opposable thumbs.
Palm pads to buttress rifles and blades
my softness used to bludgeon
my softness used to cleave.'

The implement is clamped
against the hypothenar fat pad
stiffened by contraction
of the palmaris brevis muscle.

You lick a fingertip, turn a page
flick an itch from your ankle.

I close the page
fold his face
drop him to the floor.

I reach for you
pad my fingertips over creases
in the spongy saddle of your thumb.

My blood shimmers
when you touch my face
with a pressure light as petals.

How much
do you hold back
distilled in fingertips?

Your hands
conspiring to do nothing more
than quicken my pulse.

Hues

As the Tower Belle eased us
from the clutch of the bank
we breathed a fusion of greens.

Unpicked from the green weave
its prow nuzzled water into ripples
and the bank began to blur.

One lady wanted plant names
tried to unpick the green weave
another wanted place names
another the species of birds

but we dared to blur
to breathe a fusion of greens.

We didn't want words
only a rush of green
the world blurred smooth
as the Tower Belle eased us through.

We let nothing cling
shed skin after skin.

We would return to names
but for one afternoon
we longed to slur
let our skins slick
smooth through green hues.

We let cities blur, forests slide
gave farms and fields the slip.

Piano

Each year, the tuner arrived.

We watched him bow over the soundboard
unscrewing hammers with flattened heads.

He wiped the wires, wrapped them in felt,
capped pins with a wrench, twisted,
flicked his fork, picked a string,

listening, tightening
until sprung steel and prongs
sang the same note.

Every week we sat beside a tutor
with a strand of spittle
strung between her long front teeth.

None of us kept it up.

Someone lifted a loose key.
The piano stood gap-toothed.

Stalking The Poet

I.

We discuss him at the long table
bare feet seeping heat into flagstones
in a kitchen that stays cold all year.

We begin outside his window
eye his ship's figurehead
pleased to find scratches in her chest

follow minnows of light
drifting through his bottled ships
squint closer for miniature clippers
tweezered through glass necks
rigged with string
to raise masts, spars, sails
with a gentle pull.

We peruse his sea ivory
explore scrimshaw, each cut
etched into his cachalot's tooth
walrus tusk, narwhal horn
inked with needles
tipped in candle black, tobacco juice
to detail the curve of a bosom
a sperm whale's spume.

We chant the names of dead poets
carved in the beams of his mahogany bar
stare at a gypsy ball
bleared with fingerprints
chairs shaped like water lilies
a dreg of brandy
in his crystal decanter

glimpse, but do not pause
on oil portraits

ignore the lustrous women
that line the halls.

II.

His neighbour says he's headed down the street.

We spot his curiosity
shrinking on shop windows
distilling to drips

swipe lines through his breath
rub it into our skin.

A cat is still purring where he paused
for his face in the polish of its eye.

We stroke until our hands are thinly gloved
in the grease he too has worn.

There are white petals on a window
where he laid his fingers
on dimmed rooms

boot treads in the dust
resettling on a swept doorstep.

By the river
we press our palms onto crushed grass
straining to straighten its blades
where he knelt to wash his pen.

A lady ushers us into her front garden
claims he parted the folds of her old tea rose
to unspool its scent.

There is no trace of him near the upturned pot
or in the scribble of stems and spiders
he tipped onto his shadow

though we roll our sleeves
dip our arms elbow deep.

Home to the Garden Centre
The Forest of Dean

We return when the garden flares
red, pink, orange rhododendrons and camellias,
hydrangeas freeing their blue moths

to nest cones spit-stitched to the eaves,
the gargoyle with moss on his hands,
a nostril plugged with lichen.

We return to paths ribbed with sleepers,
bogey wheels spiked with cogs
rusting on stream banks

to locked coal mines,
unworked, cream-faced quarries,
a forest still oozing iron,
bedrocks greased with ore.

We return to boss-eyed boar rutting on the verge,
piglets with humbug stripes

to hunting, saltlicks, culls,
white flickers
in the tails of fallow deer.

We return to the stuccoed house,
two miners' cottages knocked through

to the stutter of her Singer
as she hems Liberty prints for curtains, cushion covers,
foot dipping, rising on the treadle.

We return to her ceramic bowl
beside the Belfast sink

shaped like a bellflower,
black with tadpoles every spring

their mouths opening holes in the surface,
their tiny sucks on our fingertips.

Blooms

While he stayed shut, her throat bloomed
long-stemmed flowers
threading their colours through a breeze
that barely wanted anything
gave petals to a wind just strong enough
to slow them as they began to sink.

She thought she had lost these purples, yellows, reds
had only the paler ones left.

10.30 To Severn Beach

She sat beside me at Montpelier station.
She said she liked to see the seasons come in.

Her ankles were threaded with dark veins.
I thought of dead wisteria still gripping bricks.

Her face was pink sacks, grey pouches
hung from ledges of bone.

She said she'd given up Clifton
high ceilings were hard to heat.

On the other side of the line
bramble stalks were dark purple.

We spoke of Brighton
propping your back on a groyne

plucking at its barnacles
sliding fingers over tiny mirrors
of black quartz

as the sea spat inky sprawls
of bladderwrack, snatched it back.

She said you get it when there's a gale.

In the morning, all those pebbles
chucked out onto the promenade

and the water whooshing over
might catch you any moment.

She'd lived in a Regency house
just the basement though

and could always hear the sea
even in the dark.

We talked of Arundel Castle – the gift shop
those lovely soaps and woollens.

She led me there with her sentence.

It's reached along a flat path
at the bottom of the village.

She stood up to go
said she didn't want to keep me.

I wanted to keep her.

I stepped through the lisp
of sliding doors.

When the 10.30 left
she was still sat on the bench.

Bechstein

Towards the end
our nights are laced with rum

tumblers shaped like bulbs
gold with Sailor Jerry's
ring-staining the lid
of your father's Bechstein

mingling with the blood in your long fingers
so you forget *Für Elise*
slur the keys
then try to kiss me
your hands wanting my waist.

I back away
when you slam the fallboard
unable to remember even the old tunes
you've kept safe in your fingers for years

feel no heat
when you test the give of my skin

or later
as you peel lace from my crotch.

I pause my eyes on the bedroom walls
noticing thicker darks
where our shadows overlap

wake at dawn
to find your hands bridged
as if playing the bed sheet.

Lizzie

I read of Dante Gabriel Rossetti
tucking a book in Lizzie's hair
Highgate, plot 5779
stowing hours spent
rhyming the planes of her face
wording her long neck
while she faded on laudanum
in 14 Chatham Place.

I understand burials
delete Word files
type an email address
in the Hotmail search box
click select all
delete
empty recycling bin
clear.

After seven years
he paid men in beer
to prise the grave slab
spade glints knifing loam
as they picked out his lyric
to her lips, her auburn hair.

I understand exhumations
recharge an old phone
slot in its Sim
for text message streams.

They plucked out his book
with a Bible and a worm
leaves edged red
bound in calfskin
disinfectant reek
when he unpeeled the rags.

I open blank documents
select, copy
emails, text messages
paste old words
to clean screens.

He chose a new typeset
edited his metaphors
for her lips
filled wormholes
with new words for her hair
tweaked his meter
to quicken her pulse.

I understand edits
delete
replace
retype
right-click for synonyms
select all
scroll for Times New Roman.

He rewrote her reds
her seductions, shames
the flames in her hair
selected new words
for medieval rooms
gleams of lattice, arras
burnt perfumes, parted damask.

I spell-check
save as
rename
print
close
shut down.

Lasagne

My face slides
reflected in oil.

I warm milk
loosen Manchego cheese.

My breath dissolves
while I stir
lean close to the sauce.

I glide an ingot of butter
across a pan
ceiling light in its train.

While he pulls a cord
turning blinds
I unwrap onions
peel white paper from garlic.

Light slants in
as saliva settles into cheap Merlot
sipped, then glugged into mince.

He works a tight window catch
opens the room
gives away our fumes.

I peg pasta
between fingers and thumbs
lay it down for him.

Christ Church with St Ewen

On the second step
the man from Slovakia
shrugs when I ask for the entrance.

He doesn't want wrought iron
gilded mahogany
Paty's cherub panels.

He doesn't want a font
carved with fern fronds
only to give up his weight.

The second step
is worn to a dip
to seat the man from Slovakia

whose eyes are wide and wet
the stone second step
supporting the man from Slovakia

while he tells me of his wife
stuck in the States
expired visas, fucked-up paperwork.

On the second step
the oak door accepts our weight.

Beneath a thousand years
the man from Slovakia rests for five minutes
lets his flesh sink, props his bones
on the second step.

Under Christ's face in low relief
a dragon weathervane
niched saints
with noses rubbed to pug

under quarter boys
striking the quarter hour

the man from Slovakia
tells me he was given bad advice
and his new wife can't get out.

His young, tired spine
presses the door.

His muscles loosen
as he is cupped in the dip
of the second step
calves stretched
over its blunt lip.

The man from Slovakia tells me
he's had enough
can't do this any more.

There is a carved oak leaf
curled near his ear
edges defined by grime.

On the second step
under Christ in low relief
the man from Slovakia.

Clear

Our new spades prise a lid of dry soil
from loam riddled with red ants, rotten bulbs
last year's hyacinths that failed to hatch
nipped and leached by microbes.

We peel away grass, trailing roots
like threadbare rugs, tear webs
beaded with orange spiders.

Brambles split bin bags
until there is only a brown slope
scraped tree roots.

We leave the magnolia intact
still generous in its second flowering.

My Black Gardens

I gather my dead.
I am the last to taste their sweetness.

I lick conches clean
suck on fingers, paws, toes.
I lose specks of myself when I salt them.

I shape my dead
take their textures
drop smoothed stones.

I nibble off the days
layering skins.
I gather egg cases, pebbles, breaths.

I give myself –
they leave in crystal pelts.
I gather the meanings my watchers give me.

I relinquish my black gardens
matted kelp, ripe bladderwrack.
I lose skins.

I give up my dead
their skins, their splintered shells.
I take pebbles.

I give up their sweetness
their bitter tangs.
I surrender egg cases.

Sometimes I drop a ship, a whale
my hugest hearts.
I grab their breaths.

I surrender my shingle
my shattered dead.
I relinquish pebbles.

Thomas' Room

after Thomas Chatterton

They have locked
Thomas' room.

For years he was a secret
kept above the North Porch.

These days
most niches are locked.

A steward spiralled me up the stairwell
cool as a conch.

These days
the tiny doors are locked.

He opened the niche
they let Thomas use

a hexagonal room glimpsing Bristol
through slit windows

light, a scattering of city
slotting into Thomas' eyes.

These days, the church's hidden hollows
are shut in black oak

replica keys sliding
into oiled locks.

For years the church tucked up its bats
its young secret above the porch

but it is harder to be a secret these days
the stone's hidden pockets are blocked.

In Thomas' room his sapling limbs
dropped white leaves to a mosaic floor

drafts of poems he signed with a medieval name
but forgeries are harder these days.

In a deep stone crease
something fluttered, settled its wings

but there are few niches now for us
and the tiniest doors are locked.

Clean

A spider trails its tiny shadow
across the bathroom tiles.
Your heat is gone but there are scents
Aramis between towel folds.

I drop a pinch of cranefly in the bin
crispy wings, bent legs
like crossed cutlery.

I swipe lines through rooms
soft with dust
lift a finger grey-capped
with you or us.

No one changes bulbs
in the IKEA moons
you hung askew
or cleans dark sediment
from their metal ribs.

There is only my shadow on the wall
fist unfurling to drip wreckage.

New paint begins to blend
Gardenia rolled over our touch.

There's still that sticky shape on the radiator.

I watch warm air rise
flick shadow threads.

Pipes click at night.

Woolworths

From those years
I choose waking to find her combing my hair.

I choose the Savoy Picture Palace
where we watched foreign films between peach walls
sulky usher in the orchestra pit

vaulted ceiling dripping small chandeliers
plaster medallions framing myths in pale oils
swags so well restored
shadows returned to their precise creases.

Beneath glinting crystal
she whispered about her body
her legs too long, lips too big.

She wore ballet pumps, waistless shifts
stick-on stars beside her eyes
Liz Taylor lips she would nibble
with her front teeth.

I choose her white house in the fields
five cold storeys
her family wearing its damp in their clothes
no telly, just an antique Grundig
easing a dial through static to reach *The Archers*

rooms bricked up with loved books
leather-bound, softened paperbacks
that slopped over your hands.

Sleeping over
I'd watch her peel away her lashes
wipe off her iconic mouth.

I choose waking to find her combing my hair
gentle tug on my scalp
furrowing of fingers and plastic teeth.

I choose apple laces slithered
from a Pick 'n' Mix bag
that crackled as she unrolled its neck
sugar sparking on our tongues.

I choose Woolworths
its plastic bazaar of sweets
scoops sunk in milk mice
strawberry lips.

Writing Him Out

She punctured the cartridge
squeezed until dark blue words
slid into the slit of the nib.

When ink stopped she wrote a bright scratch
pressed the pen tip to her tongue
moistened a clot to free one more line.

She bled the nib in a glass
swilled out dark silt.

The plughole glugged up stained water
then swallowed him down for good.

Acknowledgements

I am grateful to the following journals, in which some of these poems have appeared: '10.30 To Severn Beach' in *Southword* (April 2016); 'Christ Church with St Ewen' in *Raceme* (No. 3, 2016); 'Rivers' in *Best New British and Irish Poets 2016* (Eyewear Publishing, March 2016); 'Lizzie' in *The Interpreter's House* (Issue 62, 2016); 'Woolworths', 'Stalking The Poet' and 'Crockery' in *Agenda* (Vol. 50, Feb 2017).

The lines from 'On Raglan Road' by Patrick Kavanagh in 'Station' are reprinted by kind permission of the Trustees of the Estate of the late Katherine B. Kavanagh, through the Jonathan Williams Literary Agency.